from Poppy Seed to Me

from Poppy Seed to me

Julie Larrick

gatekeeper press
Columbus, Ohio

This book is a work of fiction. The names, characters and events in this book are the products of the author's imagination or are used fictitiously. Any similarity to real persons living or dead is coincidental and not intended by the author.

From Poppy Seed to Me
Published by Gatekeeper Press
2167 Stringtown Rd, Suite 109
Columbus, OH 43123-2989
www.GatekeeperPress.com

Copyright © 2020 by Julie Larrick

All rights reserved. Neither this book, nor any parts within it may be sold or reproduced in any form or by any electronic or mechanical means, including information storage and retrieval systems, without permission in writing from the author. The only exception is by a reviewer, who may quote short excerpts in a review.

The cover design for this book is entirely the product of the author. Gatekeeper Press did not participate in and is not responsible for any aspect of this element.

Library of Congress Control Number (LCCN): 2020943616
ISBN (hardcover): 9781662903571

From Poppy Seed to Me Instructions

This story of a developing baby was created to be customizable for each pregnancy. The beginning of each poem has a blank for the month that the corresponding development and birth of your baby took place. There are also pages that contain questions for you to enter information regarding your personal experience with pregnancy and birth.

1-4 weeks

Sometime in _____

you came to be

the size of a poppy seed

that one can barely see.

But God knew you were there, created from love,

a gift from heaven

come down from above.

So Poppy Seed, Poppy Seed, burrow in tight,

surrounded by warmth

and love's awesome might.

Size: Poppy seed
Weight: Small paperclip
Talent: Burrowing

When did you find out you were pregnant?

_____

_____

_____

What were some of your symptoms?

_____

_____

_____

Who did you tell first?

_____

_____

_____

5-8 weeks

Now it is_____

and you've grown a whole bunch,

as big as a sweet pea

and loved very much.

What is that I hear coming from love's seat?

Thump thump, thump thump -

it's your own little heartbeat.

How wonderful God made you, just follow the trail

from the top of your head

to your cute little tail.

Size: Pea
Weight: Jellybean
Talent: Heart starts beating

When did you first hear the heartbeat?
_____
_____
_____

What was your reaction to hearing the heartbeat?
_____
_____
_____

9-12 weeks

Having fun in_____

as you've grown a lot more -

a strawberry in motion

that your parents just adore.

You've added swallowing to your little bag of tricks

as you practice your karate moves -

Kick, Kick, Kick!

Mommy doesn't feel you yet, but she will soon

as you dance around and wiggle

in your little cocoon.

Size: Strawberry
Weight: Nickel
Talent: Creating tiny movements and kicking

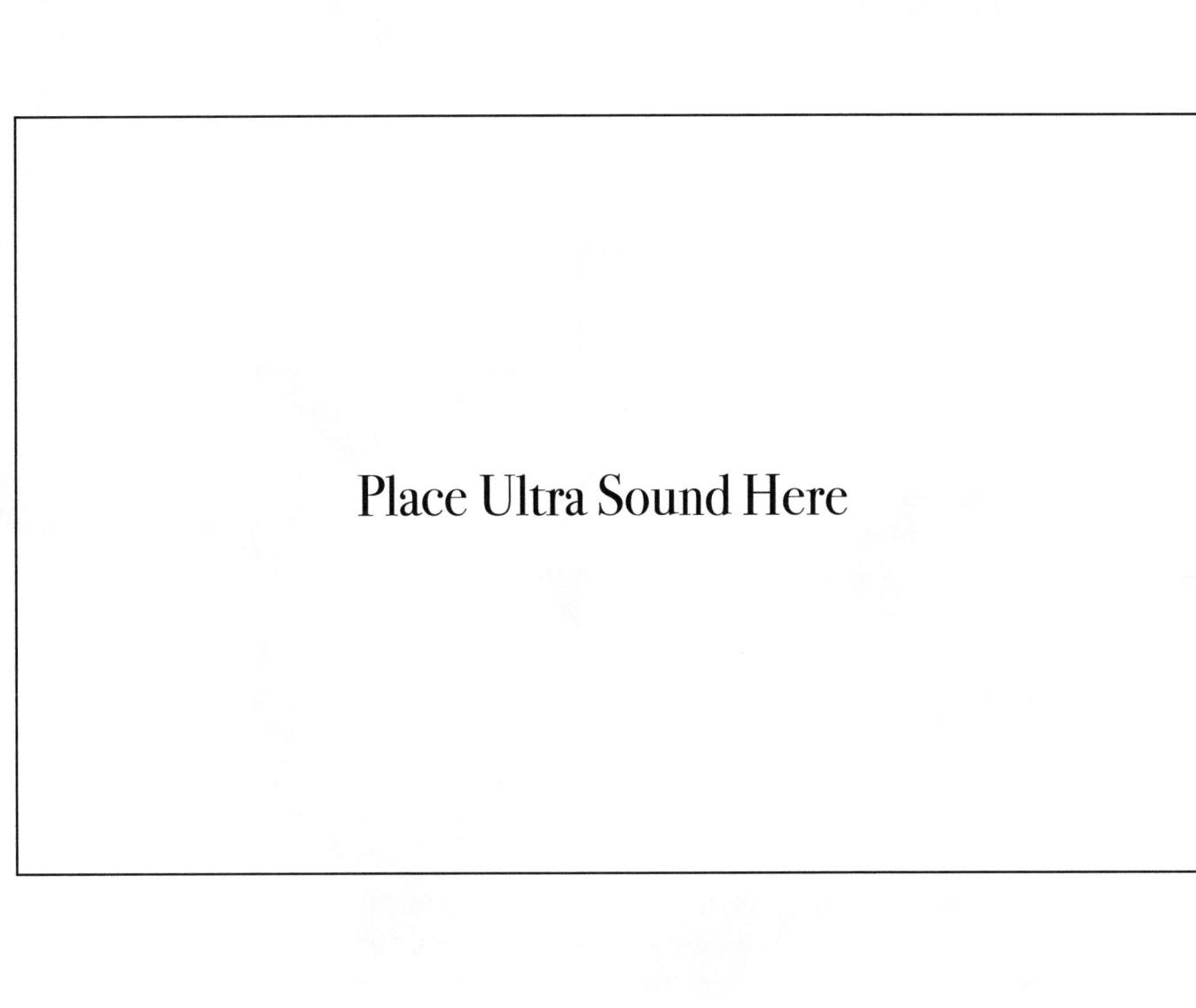

13-16 weeks

Here it is_____

and this lesson I'll teach -

how you have grown tiny hairs and

you are Mommy's fuzzy little peach.

You love stretching your fingers and wiggling your toes.

Your heart beats with excitement, yet nobody knows.

Oh, wonders of wonders, it's really the best

how you have started hearing sounds

from outside of your nest.

Size: Peach
Weight: Golf ball
Talent: Starting to hear sounds, growing fuzzy hairs called lanugo

What were some of the reactions from family and friends when finding out you were pregnant?

_____
_____
_____
_____

What were some of your symptoms in the first trimester?

_____
_____
_____
_____

17-20 weeks

_____ comes fast and you're growing up quick.

Mommy may even feel now

your tiny little kicks.

You're about the size of a sweet potato pulled from the ground,

but more precious than gold,

weighing less than a pound.

For some, it is picture time

and Mom's heart's in a twirl

as she just might find out

if you are a boy or a girl

Size: Sweet potato
Weight: Softball
Talent: Growing big enough for Mommy to know if a boy or a girl, becoming more active

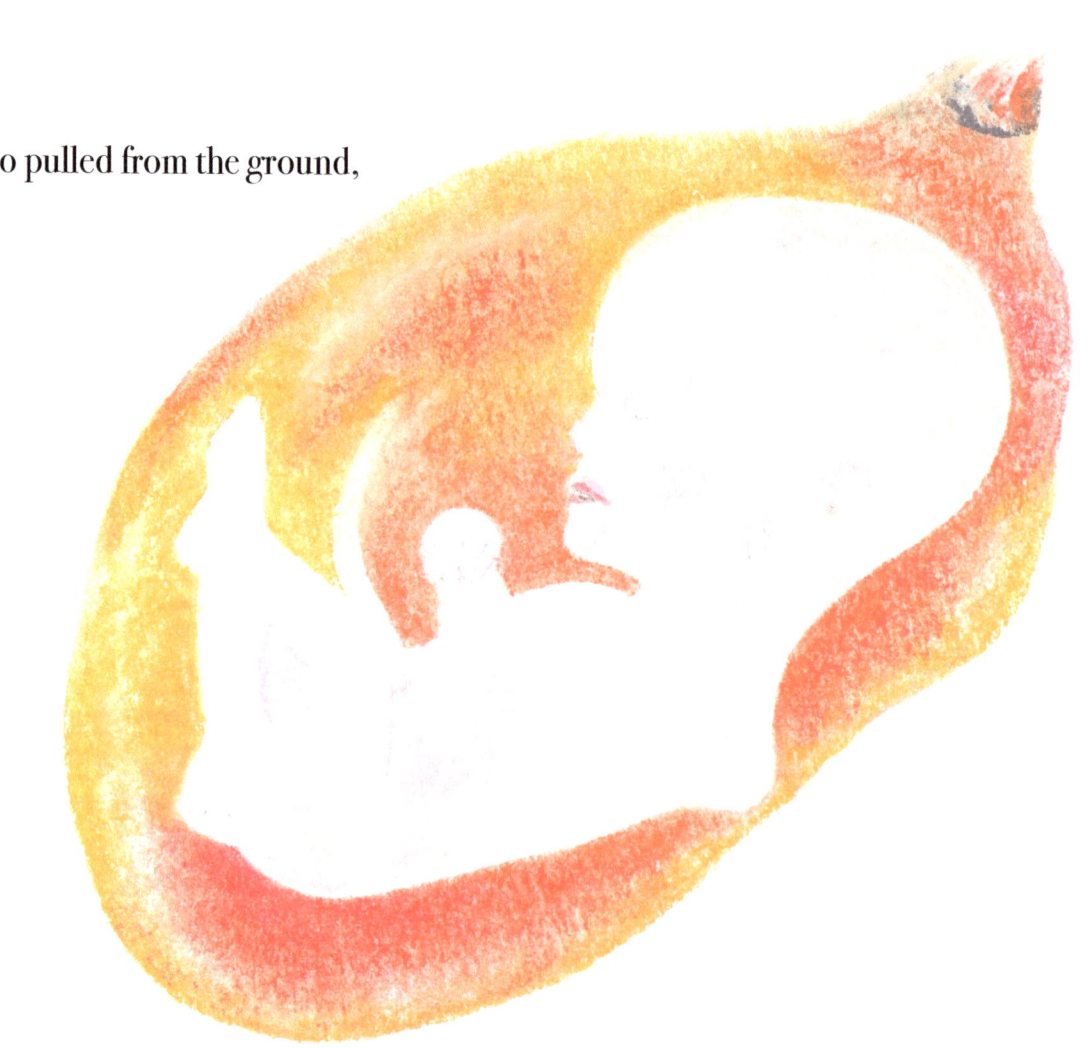

When did you first feel movement?

_____

_____

_____

What was your reaction to first feeling your baby move?

_____

_____

_____

21-24 weeks

_____ comes in, and the excitement builds.

Just thinking about seeing you

makes your parents so thrilled.

You are a small little coconut fallen from a tree.

Your eyes haven't opened yet,

but light you can see.

You like moving around and you never get bored

as you try grabbing with your hands

your belly button cord.

Size: Coconut
Weight: An umbrella
Talent: Seeing light although eyes are closed

What have you decided for a nursery theme?
_____
_____
_____

Have you decided on bottle feeding or breast feeding?
_____
_____
_____

25-28 weeks

The time is flying as _____ rolls by.

You're the size of a leaf of lettuce.

Mommy takes a deep sigh.

She is dreaming of holding you,

but you're curled up in your space.

It is a time of waiting,

a time of grace.

Your eyes are wide open as you look up and down,

and soon all will know

if those eyes are blue, green, or brown.

Size: Leaf of lettuce
Weight: A quart of water
Talent: Opening eyes

When did you find out the sex of the baby?

_____
_____
_____

How did you tell family and friends about the baby's gender?

_____
_____
_____

29-32 weeks

And so comes _____. As your mommy looks back,

she smiles knowing everything

is right on track.

Your size is perfect, like a summer squash that is yellow.

Sometimes you are active,

and sometimes you are mellow.

You hiccup, drink fluid, and move your

hands and feet to say hi,

but getting tired you fall asleep

listening to Mommy's lullaby.

Size: Yellow squash
Weight: Pineapple
Talent: Hearing more sounds,
drinking the amniotic fluid, hiccupping

What symptoms have you had in the 2nd trimester?
_____
_____
_____
_____

What plans have you made for the delivery?
_____
_____
_____
_____

33-36 weeks

_____ is here with not much time to wait,

and Mommy is hoping

that you will not be late.

You're as big as a papaya, and your home is very cramped.

You are like a letter from God

that has been addressed, sealed, and stamped.

You make one more large movement, and it's no easy stroll.

With your head pointed downward,

you are ready to roll.

Size: Papaya
Weight: A bag of sugar
Talent: Gaining weight, moving to an upside-down position

What things did you like to do to interact with your baby? (Sing songs, read, etc.)

_____
_____
_____
_____

How did your baby respond?

_____
_____
_____
_____

37-40 weeks

It's time! It's time! Your birthday is here!

The month is _____.

Get ready to cheer.

Like a watermelon going down a tunnel, but then

you open eyes to bright lights,

and you want to go back in.

You become so afraid that you let out a great cry,

but to your surprise,

everyone just sighs.

Size: Small watermelon
Weight: Average 6-8 lbs.
Talent: Going from living in a liquid environment to the outside, crying

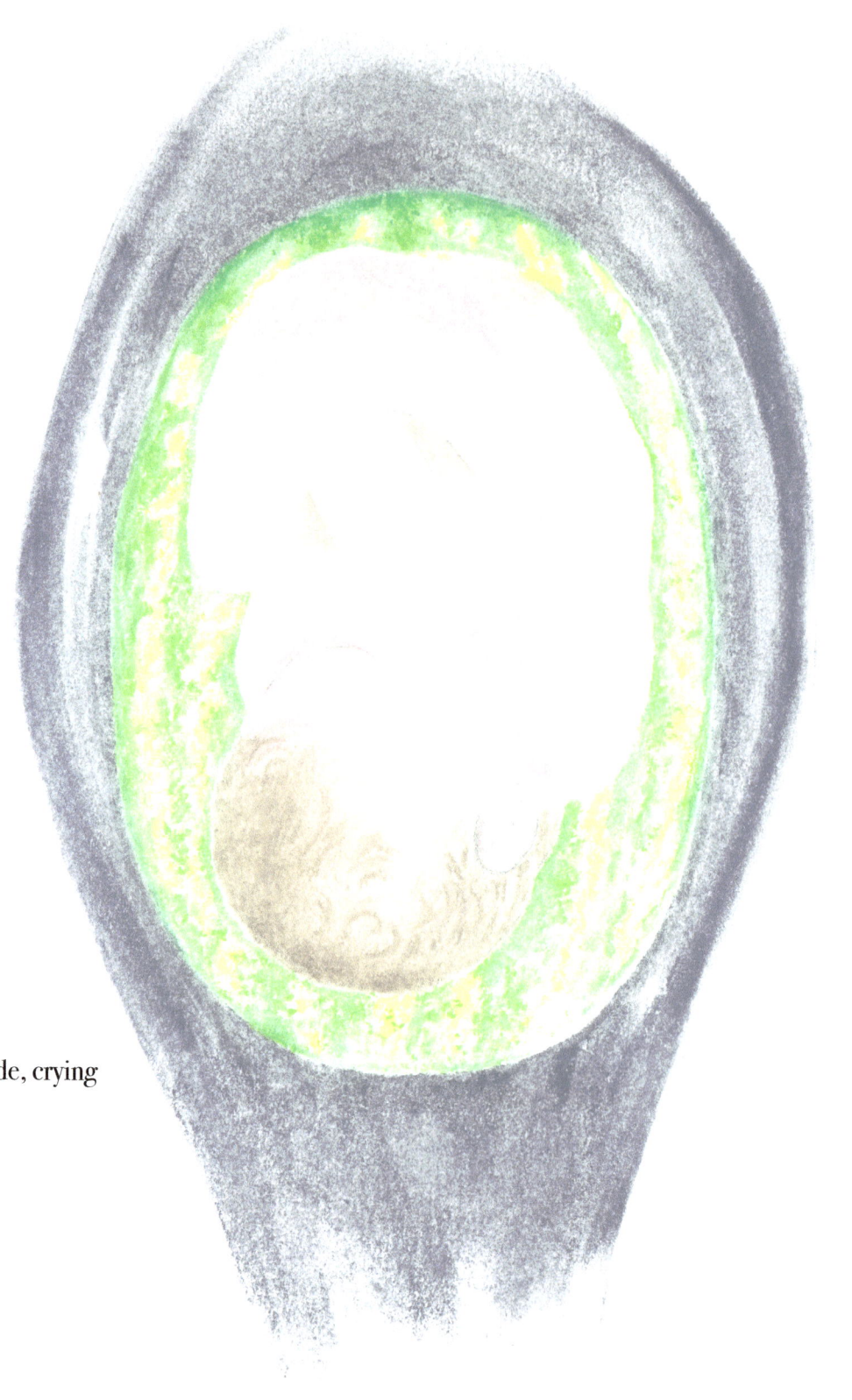

What are some names you have picked out?

_____
_____
_____
_____
_____
_____
_____
_____

Then finally, finally, with love and great care,

you're in the arms of your mommy

who says, "I love you, I love you, and I'm so glad that you're here."

From the size of a poppy seed to the size you are now,

God has molded and made you,

and just look at you - wow!

An angel from God whispers in your sweet ear,

"You have so much to do

and to see and to hear.

So just take my hand and know that you're loved

as you continue life's journey

with help from above."

The angel was right as I look back and see

how God has always been there

from Poppy Seed to me..............

Name of the Doctor/Midwife _____

Baby's Name: _____

Date of birth _____   Time _____

Weight _____   Length. _____

What family members for friends were there for the delivery or directly afterwards?

_____

_____

_____

What was the most special part of having your baby?

_____

_____

_____

Pictures

www.ingramcontent.com/pod-product-compliance
Lightning Source LLC
LaVergne TN
LVHW070408080526
838200LV00089B/365